LIFE CYCLES

The
Alligator

Published by Raintree Steck-Vaughn Publishers, an imprint of Steck-Vaughn Company.

Acknowledgments
Project Editor: Pam Wells
Design Manager: Joyce Spicer
Editor: Sabrina Crewe
Designers: Ian Winton and Steve Prosser
Consultant: Michael Chinery
Illustrator: Jim Chanell
Electronic Cover Production: Alan Klemp
Additional Electronic Production: Scott Melcer
Photography credits on page 32

Planned and produced by The Creative Publishing Company

Library of Congress Cataloging-in-Publication Data
Crewe, Sabrina
       The alligator / Sabrina Crewe ; [illustrator, Jim Chanell].
           p.   cm. — (Life cycles)
       Includes index.
       Summary: Provides an introduction to the life cycle; physical characteristics, behavior, and habitat of the American alligator.
       ISBN 0-8172-4375-5
       1. American alligator — Juvenile literature.   2. American alligator — Life cycles — Juvenile literature. [1. Alligators.]   I. Chanell, Jim, ill.   II. Title.   III. Series: Crewe, Sabrina. -Life cycles.
       QL666.C925C74   1998
       597.98 — dc21   96-53250
                                                               CIP   AC

1 2 3 4 5 6 7 8 9 0 LB 01 00 99 98 97
Printed and bound in the United States of America.

Words explained in the glossary appear in **bold** the first time they are used in the text.

The
Alligator

Sabrina Crewe

RSVP

RAINTREE
STECK-VAUGHN
PUBLISHERS
The Steck-Vaughn Company

Austin, Texas

The alligator eggs are in the nest.

It is summer. The alligator has laid her eggs in a hole on the top of her nest. Now she will cover the eggs with leaves and twigs. Inside the eggs, baby alligators are growing.

The alligator keeps guard.

The alligator watches carefully over her nest. She will stop any **predators** from taking her eggs. The eggs are kept warm by the sun and the cover of rotting plants.

The baby alligators come out of their eggs.

After about two months, the hard shell of the egg starts to crack. Under the hard shell is another, tough layer. Baby alligators use a special tooth on their **snouts** to cut through the tough layer. Then they **hatch** from their eggs.

The baby alligators are very small.

The baby alligators are only 9 inches (22 cm) long
when they hatch. They have black bodies with
pale yellow marks. The baby alligators call for
help from inside the nest. When she hears their
calls, the mother alligator uncovers the nest.

The mother alligator carries her babies.

The mother alligator scoops the babies into her large mouth. She takes them from the nest to the edge of the pool. Then she drops them in the water. The mother makes several trips to get all the babies to the pool.

The baby alligators can swim well.

Baby alligators can swim from the moment they hatch. In the water, they are safe from land animals. But they may be caught by birds, fish, or snakes.

The alligators live along a mudbank.

The mother alligator has made a hole in the mud on the side of the pool. It is a safe home for the baby alligators. When they need food, the alligators come out of the hole to swim in the pool. There they catch insects and tiny fish to eat.

The babies stay close to their mother.

Even though the babies can feed themselves, the mother alligator still takes care of them. When they come out of the pool to lie in the sun, the little alligators stay by their mother. Sometimes they lie right on top of her!

The young alligators hunt for food.

The young alligators have grown much bigger. They are safer from predators. When they are nine months old, the young alligators start to spend more time out in the pool. Now they can hunt for larger **prey**.

The young alligator has caught a crayfish.

When alligators are young, they prey mostly on animals that live in the water. They hunt for **crayfish**, fish, and frogs. They can catch small snakes and small birds, too.

The young alligator is four feet long.

The young alligator is nearly three years old.
When alligators are two or three years old,
their mothers don't look after them anymore.
Until they are five years old, young alligators
in danger still get help. Any older alligator
will come if it hears a young one call.

The young alligator loses its stripes.

The yellow stripes on the alligator's body fade as it gets older. It turns a gray color like its mother. The alligator will keep growing all its life. Alligators usually grow to about 10 feet (3 m) long. Very old alligators have reached almost 20 feet (6 m).

The alligator is very still.

Alligators do not become **mature** until they are over six years old. By this time, they can hunt much bigger animals. The alligator has seen a bird coming to the water's edge. Most of the alligator is hidden. Only the top of its head shows as it goes closer to the bird.

The alligator catches the bird.

Suddenly, the alligator grabs the bird. It pulls the bird down into deep water to drown it. The alligator does not chew its prey. Small animals are swallowed whole. Large animals are torn into pieces and then eaten.

The alligator is digging a pool.

In winter, there is not much rain where alligators live. Streams often dry up. The alligator has to dig into the ground to find water. As it digs, water fills the hole the alligator has made. The water makes a pool where the alligator can live.

The alligators lie in the sun.

Alligators become very quiet in winter. The colder weather makes them **dormant**. Most of the time they stay in their pools or in a mudbank. On sunny days, they come out to lie in the sun and warm their bodies.

The alligator is fishing.

In spring, the rain starts. There is plenty of water and food for the alligators again. The alligator is in a stream. The stream is flowing fast after a heavy rain. The alligator catches fish in its teeth by letting the water run through its mouth.

The male alligators are fighting.

Spring is also the time when alligators mate.
Male alligators will fight each other if they are
rivals for the same female. They use their tails
and sharp teeth to attack each other. The winner
will mate with the female alligator.

The alligator bellows loudly.

The male alligator makes a loud noise in his throat. From far away it sounds like thunder. The noise is the alligator's mating call. He is trying to attract the female alligator. The female answers with a quieter call.

The alligator has found a mate.

The alligators swim together before mating. They move in circles around each other for a while. Then the male grips the female with his strong jaws. He will mate with the female to **fertilize** her eggs.

The female alligator makes a nest.

Two months after mating, the female alligator finds a place near the edge of the water. She builds a mound of mud and plants to make a nest. The alligator uses her back feet to make a hole on top where she can lay her eggs.

Alligators need places with water.

For many years, alligators were hunted by people who wanted their skins. Most hunting has stopped. But now the alligators' **habitat** is in danger. People can help alligators by staying away from the wet places where they live.

Parts of an Alligator

Alligators are **crocodilians**. Crocodilians are **reptiles** with hard plates covering their bodies. They are the biggest and cleverest of reptiles. Crocodilians have strong tails for swimming and attacking prey. They are all hunters that live near water.

Teeth
Very sharp for gripping and tearing food

Throat
Flap stops water from getting in when swimming

Tail
Very powerful for swimming
and for attacking prey and
enemies

Scutes
Hard plates covering top of
the body

Back feet
Webbed with four toes

Skin
Soft and smooth on
underside of body

Other Reptiles

The alligator in this book is an American alligator. Alligators are a lot like crocodiles. You can tell which is which by their teeth. An alligator never shows more than a few of its top teeth when its mouth is closed. A crocodile shows some of its lower teeth as well, even when it closes its mouth. Here you can see another alligator and some different kinds of reptiles.

Saltwater crocodile

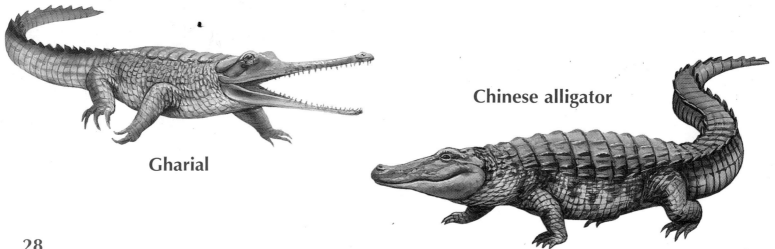

Gharial

Chinese alligator

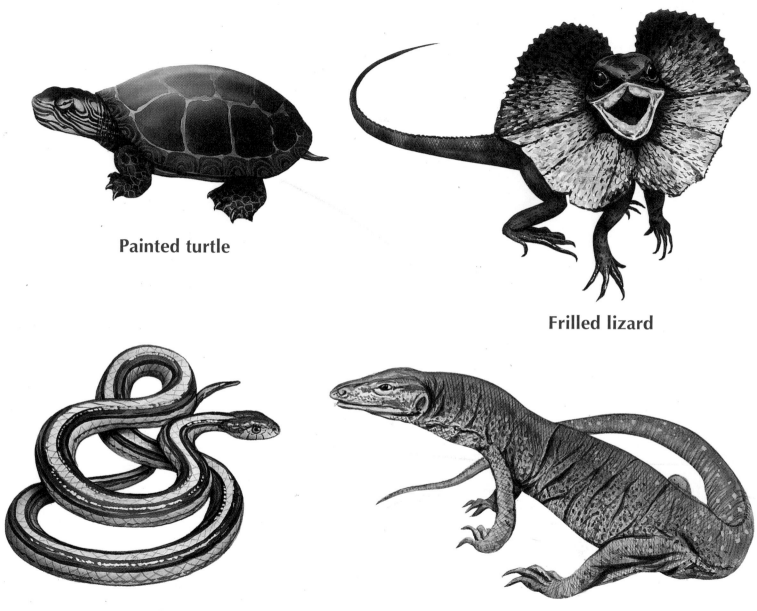

Painted turtle

Frilled lizard

Garter snake

Monitor lizard

Where the American Alligator Lives

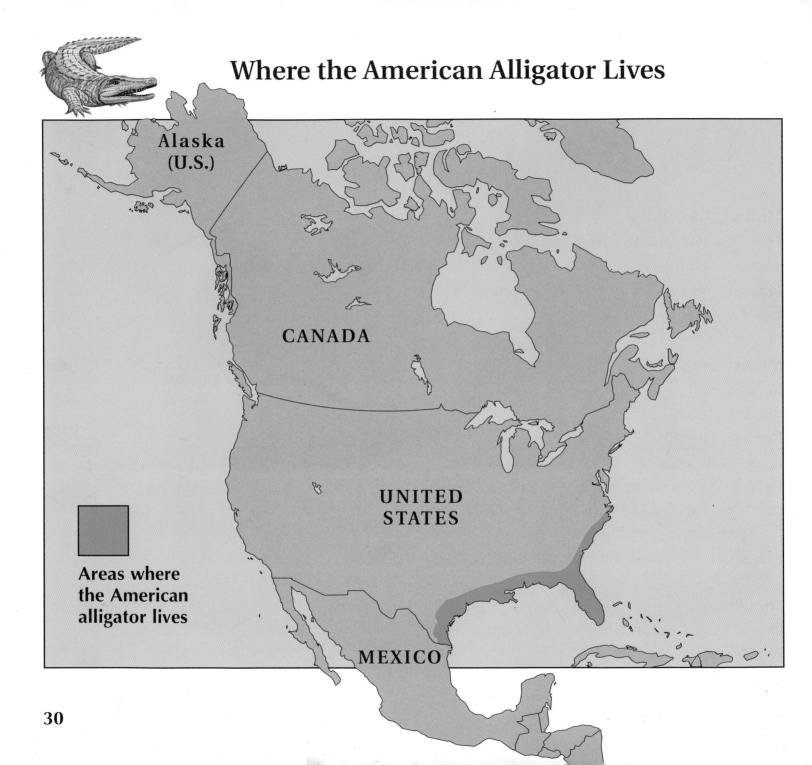

Alaska
(U.S.)

CANADA

UNITED
STATES

Areas where
the American
alligator lives

MEXICO

Glossary

Crayfish A animal that lives in water and looks like a small lobster

Crocodilian A reptile with hard plates covering its body

Dormant Asleep or not active

Fertilize To make a female's egg able to produce young

Habitat The place where an animal or plant is usually found

Hatch To come out of an egg

Mature Fully developed

Predator An animal that hunts and kills other animals for food

Prey An animal hunted or killed by another animal for food

Reptile A type of animal that lays its eggs on land and has scales or hard plates covering its body

Rival An animal or person that tries to get the same thing as another

Snout The front part of an animal's head that is made up of its nose and jaws

Index

Photography credits